# THE TALENTED TENTH

## HISTORICAL AND PRESENT: PIONEERS

### VOLUME 1

WRITTEN BY:
ASHLEY FEAZELL

ILLUSTRATED BY:
AL TARIQ HARRIS
CIARA BERLIN

# THE TALENTED TENTH

## HISTORICAL AND PRESENT: PIONEERS

### VOLUME 1

**WRITTEN BY:**
ASHLEY FEAZELL

**ILLUSTRATED BY:**
AL TARIQ HARRIS
CIARA BERLIN

www.thetalented10th.net

All rights reserved, including the right to reproduce this book or portion thereof in any form whatsoever. For information address The Talented 10th: 7806 S Harvard Blvd Los Angeles CA, 90047

Copyright © 2016 by Ashley Feazell

Paperback edition 2020

For more information about special discounts for bulk purchases, please contact ashley@thetalented10th.net or call 323-395-3787

ISBN 978-0-9994620-0-3

# INDEX

Pg. 1 Introduction
Pg. 2 George Washington Carver
Pg. 3 Henrietta Lacks
Pg. 4 Lewis H. Latimer
Pg. 5 Madam CJ Walker
Pg. 6 Benjamin Banneker
Pg. 7 Mary Davidson
Pg. 8 Granville Woods
Pg. 9 Charles Drew
Pg. 10 Elijah McCoy
Pg. 11 Garrett Morgan

# Introduction

Everyone is special. We all have certain things we can do better than others. This is our talent, and it is our responsibility to acknowledge it, and use it for good. In the Talented Tenth: Historical and Present, we will acknowledge and highlight the achievements', and talents of our culture's historical and present figures. These books will explore the vast Pan-African community and focus on its greatness. Each book will focus on 10 specific figures.

In this book The Talented Tenth: Historical and Present, one will discover Pioneers. These 10 figures have paved the way for the Pan-African community today. These figures, being inventors, entrepreneurs, strategist, doctors, and philanthropist helped many Pan-Africans achieve dreams, and better living qualities. Through great achievements, they each created hope in a community that desperately needed it. Bringing attention to themselves through good deed, and achievement, they uplifted a whole community with pride.

# George Washington Carver
**1864-1943**

George Washington Carver was born in 1864, in Diamond Missouri, born to two slaves during the civil war. On the Carver plantation, when the civil war was over, George stayed and was raised by his former masters-taught to read and write by the house's mistress because he couldn't attend school due to his race.

Carver left home to get a better education and was able to graduate from high school. Accepted into a college, but upon them learning his race, he couldn't attend, so he was left to do scientific experiments. He eventually enrolled in a botany program at Iowa State; he was the first black student. He was hired by Booker T Washington to run Tuskegee's agriculture department. In this role, Carver helped the local farmer learn how to keep cash crops. He also invented more than 300 products from the peanut, and 118 from the sweet potato. Some include soap, ink, cosmetics, and milk, to name a few. He found valuable uses for soybean and Alabama clay. Thomas Edison, intrigued by Washington, employed his services for war time inventions, making peanut rubber for World War II canons. Washington also advised Mahatma Gandhi on nutritional matters. He is the first African American man to be honored with a national monument.

George Washington Carver is one of the most famous scientists ever to walk American soil, inventing countless ways to use the peanut.

# Henrietta Lacks
1920-1951

Henrietta Lacks was born Loretta Pleasant, August 1, 1920, in Roanoke, Virginia. When her mother died, she lived with her grandfather and cousin on an old slave plantation. She became Henrietta, also romantically involved with David. They had two children before moving to Maryland, and there they had three more children. One child placed in an insane asylum due to her being mentally disabled.

Lacks went to the hospital complaining of stomach pain and diagnosed with cervical cancer. Her cells stolen for observation while being treated, and the doctors noticed her cells could survive much longer than the normal cell. She died on October 4, 1951, but doctors continued using her cells for research. Unbeknownst to her or her family, Lacks cells healthier than others; they also reproduced. Lacks' body produced the first known immortal cells, her cells survived and reproduced outside of her body. The HeLa cells used to help cure polio and HPV.

HeLa cells used to make many vaccines, over 10,000. The immortal cells of Henrietta Lacks have saved countless lives and continuously used for research to date.

# Lewis H. Latimer
### 1848-1928

On September 4, 1848, Lewis Howard Latimer was born in Chelsea, Massachusetts, born to two runaway slaves. His father's master followed them north and tried to take his father, George, back into slavery. His father was able to secure his freedom with the money and help of abolitionist Frederick Douglass. Shortly after the Dred Scott decision, his father left, most likely to keep from being sold back into slavery. Lewis, a smart child with love for drawing, had to work to help take care of his family once his father left. He enlisted in the civil war but was honorably discharged and went back to Boston to work in a patent office.

Latimer became a draftsman at the patent office, and this position gave him access to many inventors. He became friends and a valuable partner to Alexander Graham Bell and drafted the patent for the telephone. Bell's patent was established just hours before his rivals, thanks to the drawing expertise of Latimer. He worked for Thomas Edison's rival Hiram Maxim and improved the light bulb, which caught the attention of Thomas Edison, and he offered Latimer a position in his company. Latimer became part of the 'Edison Pioneers." He wrote the first book on electric lighting, "Incandescent Electric Lighting," and supervised the street lighting of major cities like London, New York, and Philadelphia. He patented inventions of his own, improving the railroad car bathroom, and even an early version of an air conditioner. Latimer worked for General Electric's legal department, becoming a patent consultant for law firms. We will never know the full extent to what Latimer invented, but his achievements are remarkable for the times he lived.

Pre and Post civil war were hard times for a black person in America, Latimer was able to create a legacy when people of his color didn't even have a voice, a true icon.

# Madam C J Walker
**1867-1919**

In Delta, Louisiana, Madam C.J. Walker was born Sarah Breedlove on December 23, 1867 on a cotton plantation to recently freed black parents. Walker was one of six children and the first in her family to be born free. She married at a young age, due to being orphaned by her parents' death, and had a daughter with her first husband. Her husband died, and she moved to St. Louis, where her brothers were barbers.

Walker got a job as a wash girl, and although she didn't make much money, she was determined to create a better future for her daughter, A'lelia. Due to her hair problems, she wanted to understand haircare. She attended classes to understand formulas to make hair creams and started working for an entrepreneur Annie Malone. Malone, an entrepreneur of hair products, explained hair care to Walker. She married a newspaper ad salesman Charles Joseph Walker and became Madam C.J. Walker, an independent hairdresser and a seller of creams, business skyrocketed. Together they created successful ad campaigns and marketing tools to promote her products. Her Glossine hair cream and the new wide-tooth pressing comb she made had business soaring. Walker left her daughter home to run the mail-order business, and Walker and her husband traveled the east, and south, teaching and recruiting women. She opened the Madam C. J. Walker Manufacturing Company and Lelia College of Beauty Culture. The companies provided thousands of African American women with jobs and career opportunities, other than a maid and wash girl. Walker even traveled the Caribbean and Central America to expand the business. She was an avid philanthropist donating funds to the YMCA in Indianapolis, and the NAACP anti-lynching fund, she even helped to preserve the Washington D.C. home of Frederick Douglass. Walker settled and purchased a New York mansion named Villa Lewaro; it is now a national historic landmark.

Madam C.J. Walker is said to be the first woman, self-made, millionaire. She was not only a teacher, but she also gave to help others achieve their life goals. Madam C. J. Walker and American Pioneer.

# Benjamin Banneker
### 1731-1806

Benjamin Banneker was born to free black parents in Baltimore, Maryland, on November 9, 1731. His mother, a mixed woman, born to an Englishwoman and a West African ex-slave. Banneker's maternal grandfather claimed to be of West African royalty.

At the age of 22, Banneker constructed a wall clock that he made after a pocket watch, which calculated accurate time, and worked for fifty years until his death and built an irrigation system for the family farm. He improved on the almanac with astrological accuracy, precisely forecasting solar and lunar eclipses. Banneker ran a tobacco farm and began publishing his almanacs. He published material including literature, astronomical calculations, opinion samples, and tidal information for fishermen, for six years. Banneker, recruited by Andrew Ellicott, became part of the team that constructed the city's layout, Washington D.C. Also, a consultant to many US Presidents on improving race relations, including George Washington and Thomas Jefferson. The correspondence between Banneker and Jefferson published in Banneker's 1793 almanac.

Benjamin Banneker lived a life not afforded to many black Americans. The freedoms he experienced were rare, but his achievements helped people see African Americans as equal and more than capable. Benjamin Banneker, an American architect.

# Mary Davidson
1912-2006

Mary Beatrice Davidson was born May 12, 1912, in Monroe, North Carolina. She comes from a family of inventors. Her father holds three patents, and her grandfather a couple as well. Growing up, her father and sister encouraged her love of inventing. She attended Howard University but eventually dropped out due to lack of funds.

Davidson's love for inventing never faded. She worked for the federal government, married James 'Jabbo' Kenner, and continued to create in spare time. In 1956 Mary and her sister developed a device that sits around the waist and clips onto a pad. The invention was to keep the pad from moving. She improved her design three years later when she created a 'moisture-proof pocket,' which went under the pad to prevent spillage on clothes. Mary didn't benefit from this invention because of her skin color, even though big brands incorporated the technology. The sanitary belt used until the stick-on invented in the 1970s.

Davidson opened a florist shop and continued to invent. Winning patents for a wheelchair tray and toilet-paper dispenser, she holds five different patents the most of any African-American woman.

# Granville Woods
### 1856-1910

Granville Woods was born on April 23, 1856, in Columbus, Ohio, to free parents. He didn't have much of a formal education growing up and left school around age ten.

Woods did various jobs, including engineering on a ship, a railroad machine shop, a steel mill, a fireman, and a railroad worker. He took courses in engineering and electronics in his spare time. Woods invented a device that allowed moving trains to communicate with each other, and the train station, preventing collisions. He also developed the trolley and a system that paved the way for the subway. Woods also created an improvement of the automatic air brake and invented the third rail, which he used on the Figure Eight, the roller coaster. Holding almost sixty patents, and most designs for the electric railway, his invention the "telegraphony" helped telegraph stations to send voice and telegraph messages over one wire and purchased by Alexander Graham Bell. Woods won a court battle brought against him by Thomas Edison over the multiplex telegraph invention. Once Edison lost, he offered Woods a position at his company to which Woods declined and instead formed Woods Electric Co.

Woods' moniker, Black Thomas Edison, made him famous, but his inventions deserved independent recognition. Granville Woods, an engineering pioneer.

# Charles Drew
### 1904-1950

Charles Richard Drew was born in Washington, D.C., on June 3, 1903. His father laid carpet for a living, and Drew was the eldest son. An athletic child he excelled in sports and earned a scholarship to Amherst College where he established himself as a track and football star.

Once he earned his bachelor's degree, he needed more funds to pursue his dream of becoming a medical doctor. He worked at Morgan College now Morgan State University as a biology instructor and coach. Once he earned enough money, he enrolled at McGill University in Montreal, Canada. At the top of his class, Drew earned accolades and became a member of the Alpha Omega Alpha medical honors society. He earned both Doctorate of Medicine and Master of Surgery degrees in Canada also completed his residency there. At this time, he studied extensively on blood storage and transfusions. Drew returned to the states after his father's death and taught medicine at Howard University. He worked at the Freedman's Hospital and taught at the university. Charles earned a Rockefeller scholarship, which allowed him to study at Columbia University and train at the New York-Presbyterian Hospital. He further explored blood-related matters and invented a method to store blood plasma with or without cells. Drew studied this thesis for his doctorate and earned his degree in 1940, making him the first African American to earn a doctorate from Columbia University. He successfully conducted and oversaw the first large blood bank drive "Blood for Britain" and the second for the American Red Cross during World War II. Drew worked on a blood bank for the US military but withdrew when he realized African American blood required segregation. He returned to teaching and became the first African American examiner for the American Board of Surgery. Drew died in a car crash at the age of forty-five.

Charles Drew is named the father of the blood bank. His studies and experiments have saved countless lives.

# Elijah McCoy
1844-1929

Elijah McCoy was born on May 2, 1844, in Ontario, Canada. His parents were fugitive slaves that fled Kentucky using the underground railroad. They returned to America shortly after his birth and settled in Michigan.

McCoy had a talent and interest for mechanics at a young age compelling his parents to send him abroad to Scotland. There he apprenticed to be an engineer. Upon returning to the states, finding an engineering job proved difficult, so he settled for a job as a railroad man. The assignment helped him develop his oiling cup invention. Before this invention, it was men's job to oil the parts of a train, McCoy's invention lubricated the components independently and without the train stopping. He focused on dependability rather than mass production. His reliable devices shaped consumer search for products, requiring "the real McCoy" instead of his competitors' versions. He formed the McCoy Manufacturing Company and primarily focused on inventing lubricating systems.

Elijah McCoy holds close to sixty patents, from lubricating systems, ironing boards, and lawn sprinklers. His lack of capital prevented him from receiving major credit, but his inventions were so trustworthy his name became infamous.

# Garrett Morgan
1877-1963

Garrett Augustus Morgan was boring March 4, 1877, in Paris, Kentucky. His mother of African and Indian descent, his father Sydney, was the freed mixed-race son of confederate colonel John Hunt Morgan.

Garrett left home as a teen with only an elementary school education. He found work as a handyman and paid for tutoring. Morgan started working as a sewing machine repairman and learned the inner workings of the machine. He received a patent for an improved sewing machine and opened his repair shop. He also created a hair straightener and opened the G.A. Morgan Hair Refining Company. This product gave Morgan financial freedom. In 1914 he patented a form of a gas mask or safety hood made for firefighters and miners. He worked tirelessly to promote the device in the south, even hiring a white man to pose as the hood's inventor while he acted as a sidekick and demonstrated the mask's ability. In 1916 an accident happened in Cleveland, Ohio, leaving miners trapped underground inhaling toxic fumes. Rescuers died breathing in the bad air. Morgan went to rescue the miners with his brother's help; they saved two lives and recovered four bodies. Once people realized he was a black man, sales for his safety hood plummeted. Despite sales reduction and lack of recognition from his heroic efforts, Garrett continued inventing. He invented a stoplight after witnessing a horrible traffic accident in the city. Many of his inventions are basic versions of the ones we use today.

Morgan's inventions helped save many lives. His stop light is a prototype of the three-way light signal we use, and his gas mask used to aid in creating the gas masks used in World War II. Garrett Morgan and American hero.

1. Where was Madam C.J. Walker born?

a. Delta, Louisiana

b. United, Louisiana

c. New Orleans, Louisiana

## 2. What is Benjamin Banneker most noted for improving?

a. Clock

b. Almanac

c. All of the above

## 3. Lewis Latimer helped draft which Alexander Graham Bell invention?

a. Light bulb

b. air conditioner

c. telephone

## 4. What did George Washington Carver use to invent over 300 products?

a. Sweet potato

b. grapes

c. peanut

# 5. Henrietta lacks has what type of cells?

a. dead

b. immortal

c. black

# 6. Garrett Morgan helped save miners using which invention?

a. gas mask

b. Submarine

c. trolley

## 7. Mary Davidson patent which invention for women?

a. Foundation

b. pantyhose

c. sanitary napkin

8. Charles Drew is the father of which currently used medical practice?

a. Blood transfusion

b. blood bank

c. vaccinations

# 9. Granville Woods was compared to which inventor?

a. Alexander Graham Bell

b. Thomas Edison

c. Benjamin Franklin

**10. Elijah McCoy's invention was so dependable it coined which phrase?**

a. "the real McCoy"

b. "not like the McCoy"

c. "only if its McCoy"

# Glossary

- **Acknowledge**: to say that you accept or do not deny the truth or existence of something (verb)
- **Align**: to array on the side of or against a party or cause (verb)
- **Almanac**: a book published every year that contains facts about the movements of the sun and moon, changes in the tides, and information of general interest (noun)

- **Dred-scot**: as an enslaved African American man in the United States who unsuccessfully sued for his freedom and that of his wife and their two daughters in the *Dred Scott v. Sandford* case of 1857 (noun)
- **Endeavor**: to work with set purpose (verb)
- **Finance**: the obtaining of funds or capital (verb)
- **Icon**: an object of uncritical devotion (noun)
- **Invent**: to devise by thinking (verb)
- **Patent**: protected by a trademark or a brand name so as to establish proprietary rights analogous to those conveyed by letters patent or a patent (noun)

- **Perseverance:** continued effort to do or achieve something despite difficulties, failure, or opposition : the action or condition or an instance (verb)

- **Philanthropist:** one who makes an active effort to promote human welfare : a person who practices (noun)

- **Sharecropper:** a tenant farmer especially in the southern U.S. who is provided with credit for seed, tools, living quarters, and food, who works the land, and who receives an agreed share of the value of the crop minus charges (noun)

Blackinventor.com
Brittanica.com
Thehistorymakers.com
Biography.com

www.ingramcontent.com/pod-product-compliance
Lightning Source LLC
Chambersburg PA
CBHW080415300426
44113CB00015B/2529